How to Create P
for Education

CW00972402

How to Create Podcasts for Education

Gilly Salmon, Palitha Edirisingha, Matthew Mobbs, Richard Mobbs, Chris Dennett

Open University Press
McGraw-Hill Education
McGraw-Hill House
Shoppenhangers Road
Maidenhead
Berkshire
England
SL6 2QL

email: enquiries@openup.co.uk
world wide web: www.openup.co.uk

and Two Penn Plaza, New York, NY 10121–2289, USA

First published 2008

A catalogue record of this book is available from the British Library

ISBN-13: 978 0 335 23534 6 (pb)
ISBN-10 0 335 23534 4 (pb)

Library of Congress Cataloging-in-Publication Data
CIP data has been applied for

Typeset by RefineCatch Limited, Bungay, Suffolk
Printed in the UK by Bell and Bain Ltd, Glasgow

Fictitious names of companies, products, people, characters and/or data that may be
used herein (in case studies or in examples) are not intended to represent any real
individual, company, product or event.

The McGraw·Hill Companies

Contents

For Noemi and Mandy – more podcasters of the future.

"While the book is a mine of information, both pedagogical and practical, it is the hands-on aspect that captured my heart. Clearly written by experts, the process of creating podcasts is described in an easy-to-understand, practical way that is accessible to novice and experienced podcast author alike … If you've been toying with the idea of podcasts, this is for you. If you've tried the basics and want to go the next step, this is for you. How to create Podcasts for Education will not merely be on your bookshelf; I predict that it will be well-thumbed!"

- **Ruth Brown**, Academic Developer, Learning and Teaching Enhancement Unit, London South Bank University, UK.

Become a Pod Author . . .

Podcasting for learning moved over our horizon early in 2006 and we started trying it out. Neither of us had tried it before. Then we noticed a surge of interest from colleagues from different disciplines and professions in the use of downloadable audio files. And we watched hundreds of students walking around our campus, sitting on the buses, or lying on the grass in the park, with MP3 players 'glued' to their ears. What previously appeared to be a somewhat 'techie' approach to playing music suddenly looked, to us anyway, like something that might have high value and low cost for learning.

This book emerges from our first attempts and the subsequent workshops and support that our team offered to others and the impact on hundreds of students. We realized that creating and distributing podcasts was pretty easy and most teachers can try it out for themselves with little help. We hope this little book will help you get started. Let us know how you get on!

If you'd like to know more about podcasting for education, please look on our research site: IMPALA (impala.ac.uk Informal Mobile Podcasting and Learning Adaptation) and our companion book site: podcastingforlearning.com. There are some example podcasts for learning on there too.

Gilly Salmon & Palitha Edirisingha,
University of Leicester, UK.

1

Podcasting technology

Based on source material from Gilly Salmon, Richard Mobbs,
Palitha Edirisingha and Chris Dennett

Summary

We begin by explaining the technology and terminology – for non-technical
readers – that enable podcasts and podcasting to happen. We also clarify the
technical characteristics that have made podcasting attractive for learning.

Definitions

The terms 'podcast' and 'podcasting' are new and evolving, but there are
working definitions that we use in this book.

We are treating 'podcast' as a noun. A podcast is a digital media file
that:

- plays audio (sound) or audio and vision (sound and something to view);
  with vision, the term 'vodcast' is sometimes used;
- is made available from a website;
- can be opened and/or downloaded (taken from the website offering it
  and placed on something of your own) and played on a computer; and/or
- is downloaded from a website to be played on a small portable player
  designed to play the sound and/or vision.

We are treating the term 'podcasting' as a verb. Podcasting is the action of:

- creating the podcast; and
- distributing the podcast.

Most audio podcasts are put into a format called 'MP3'. MP3 stands for
MPEG Audio Layer III, a standard for compressing the file to make it more
usable. Most podcasts with vision are put into a format called 'MP4'. This is a
bit like saying '.doc' for a Microsoft Word document or '.ppt' for PowerPoint
files. Just as you would need a piece of software on your computer for using
the .doc document or the .ppt one, so you need a media 'player' software for

your MP3 and MP4 files. Most of the software is available as free downloads or provided with your computer.

The Sony Walkman was probably the first device designed for personal and portable audio listening but the iPod, and its associated iTunes software, was the first small personal portable device that provided for downloading and playing podcasts. There are now many other providers of personal players at low to high prices. We suggest you look at Amazon or any review site to see the wide range of options. They are usually called 'MP3' or 'MP4' players. Used in this way, the term means the small portable device rather than the software.

The birth of pedagogical podcasting

Podcasts and podcasting were born early in the millennium. Podcasting developed because new web-based technologies could distribute and provide mass access to ('cast') audio files, and because small personal devices for playing audio were becoming widely available at a declining cost. The visual aspects came a little later.

Internet radio show hosts were quick to embrace the technologies as well as the practice of creating, distributing and accessing what were at first known as 'audio-blogs' (sound-based web-logs). To start with there was limited interest and podcasting had humble beginnings: the public was unaware of either the word or the activity. Early in 2004 the word 'podcasting' was coined by Ben Hammersley writing in *The Guardian*, a UK-based newspaper: he used it to identify the emerging practice of 'portable listening to audio-blogs' on the most popular and available audio player at the time: the iPod. In September 2004, the word 'podcast' attracted only 24 hits on Google, but by 2005 *The New Oxford American Dictionary* recognized podcasting as the 'word of the year'. By 2007, podcasting was recognized as a 'low-threshold' technology with the start of its exploration as a learning technology.

So podcasts and podcasting began as entertainment and information. The technologies involved were not designed or intended as learning technologies but, attracted by the simplicity and increasing student ownership of iPods and other makes of player, universities became interested. Duke University in the USA was one of the first into the field. Duke gave iPods to new students in October 2004 and encouraged its academic staff to explore learning and teaching applications of podcasting.

In the UK, individual academics such as Dr Bill Ashraf at Bradford University first hit the news media for podcasting his lectures in 2006. We believe that the Informal Mobile Podcasting And Learning Adaptation (IMPALA) project, which commenced in June 2006, was the first funded research project to address podcasting for pedagogical purposes in the UK. The Association of Learning Technologies Conference in September 2007 included 12 papers and posters specifically about podcasting and many more where podcasts were mentioned as part of Web 2.0.

Types of podcasts

There are three categories of podcast: audio, video and enhanced. These categories refer to the type of media file contained in the podcast.

- Audio podcasts contain sound only.
- Video podcasts contain sound and imagery, such as moving and still pictures.
- Enhanced podcasts are an extended version of audio podcasts capable of displaying additional information such as still images, weblinks and chapter markers.

Each type has its own special qualities, requirements and benefits. Here are some of the characteristics of and differences between the three categories.

Audio podcasts

Audio podcasts are the simplest of the three to create, requiring only a microphone plus recording and possibly editing software.

Of the three, an audio-only podcast takes up the smallest storage space on the computer that provides it for downloading, and on the personal devices that make it portable. Conversion utilities, which are small pieces of software, are sometimes used to reduce the size of the podcast file, thus increasing the speed of transmission and lowering the amount of storage space required. These utilities enable users to store more podcasts on their personal device.

There is a choice of recording and editing software for creating podcasts. You can choose depending on which is best for the operating system on your computer, the cost of the software and its ease of use. Very powerful free programmes are available for all the most commonly used operating systems, including Linux, Microsoft Windows and Apple computers.

Audio podcasts are available in an array of formats. The commonest one, called MP3, works on most personal players and is therefore usually the most accessible format. You will often hear devices for playing audio called MP3 players. You will hear about other formats too – Windows Media Audio (.WMA) from Microsoft (Microsoft 2004) and Advanced Audio Coding (.AAC) from Apple (ISMA 2005).

There are choices to be made because the better the quality of the sound reproduction, the greater the file size. The process by which raw audio is stored as digital information on a computer involves taking 'samples' of the analogue waveform. The more samples taken per second, the more accurate the representation of the original sound 'waveform' and the larger the file size on the computer. Formats such as MP3 use algorithms of various qualities and efficiencies to reduce the size of these files, with little effect on sound quality. The conversion utilities mentioned earlier reduce the size of MP3 sound files by setting the amount of information permitted per second.

Table 1.1 File size and sound quality

File format	File size	Example application
Raw audio data	125.7Mb	Not for podcasting
.mp3 128kbit/sec Stereo	2.6MB	Good quality music for distribution to various personal devices
.mp3 56kbit/sec Stereo	1.1MB	Voice
.m4a Automatic iTunes conversion at 128kbit/sec	2.6MB	Good quality video for distribution to iPods

This setting is referred to as the 'bit-rate' of the file and you will probably hear the term used about the quality of sound files.

Video podcasts

Video podcasts include sound and video materials. They are often called vodcasts and vodcasting. Originally, video podcasts were intended to be played on devices with larger displays, such as PCs. Earlier, the smaller devices had poor screen resolution and limited file storage. Mobile video players are now becoming popular and movie play features are often integrated into other devices such as Personal Digital Assistants (PDAs).

Video podcasts are more complicated, time-consuming and therefore a little more expensive to create. You will need:

- *Digital video cameras* come in a variety of formats, prices and output qualities and you will need one for recording your video. You can even use a webcam which is an inexpensive, simple video camera, that sits on top of your computer monitor. The cost of webcam equipment is quite low but the video quality may be poor. Professional cameras in professional hands of course produce the best results.
- *Software for editing* is essential for editing your recording, to get it to look and sound how you want. Professional video editing software is expensive and complicated, but there is some good licensed software for both Microsoft Windows and Apple computers within both their operating systems (see below).

If you decide video podcasts might be useful for your teaching and learning, you could experiment with minimal financial outlay for basic equipment.

- *The file size and format* you choose for your video podcast is more critical than for audio podcasts. Video is stored in a similar way to audio, but much more digital information is needed to include colour, brightness and contrast. The commonest format is called MP4, though there are many others, the names of some of which look similar.

- *Access* to software and players is essential for your students so they can access MP4 files. Since MP4 files tend to be much larger than audio files, students will require high-speed broadband internet access for downloading them.

Enhanced podcasts

Enhanced podcasts are audio podcasts with additional 'built-in' functions to aid the listener. One example of a built-in function is a small slide-show with its own audio commentary. Another example is podcasts split into 'chapters' by offering points within the audio track for students to 'jump to' to aid their 'navigation' and replay certain sections.

If you have some experience of creating audio podcasts and want to offer more support to your learners, enhancing podcasts is a fairly easy and cheap way of adding value. But currently there are some software and technical restrictions for creating and playing back enhanced podcasts.

Enhanced podcasts are usually produced using Apple computers, equipped with appropriate software, such as GarageBand. For playing them your students must have access to Apple's Quicktime player or iTunes software and an actual iPod, not any other make of MP3 player.

Microsoft are responding to Apple with their own 'solution' to enhance podcasting. Currently, audio and video files can be synchronized with Microsoft Producer, which is a free add-on for Microsoft PowerPoint. An alternative is to use Microsoft Movie Maker which is part of the Windows operating system. Movie Maker allows for the integration of images at pre-defined points on an imported pre-recorded audio file. Both Producer and Movie Maker produce output files with the limitation that they are only viewable using Microsoft Internet Explorer software.

Microsoft Windows Media files can be viewed on PDAs running the Windows Mobile operating system but are inaccessible via other devices such as the iPod. However, free software from Videora (videora.com) converts most of the popular multi-media files to formats suitable for viewing on the iPod.

Commercial software is available for producing enhanced podcasts from Kudlian Soft (kudlian.net). 'Podcaster' software is available for both the Apple and Microsoft operating systems and cost less than $30; it requires no more additional hardware than that discussed above. 'Podcaster' allows the addition of subtitles to images, to improve accessibility, and hyperlinks can be embedded to direct students to documents on the institutional Virtual Learning Environment (VLE), web pages on the internet or to other podcasts.

We expect that some of these restrictions will be removed before long, so it is worth checking the current position when you are ready to give enhancing a try.

Creating enhanced podcasts is only slightly more complicated than doing so for audio podcasts. Recording the audio part is the same as usual. Adding graphics involves 'dragging and dropping' slides, photographs or other static material into your chosen software tool, matching the image on screen to the right point in the audio track and typing in subtitles and hyperlinks in a separate area. The cost of creating enhanced podcasts is therefore a little more than audio, but you may feel that the podcasts become better paced and can be more easily embedded in other learning materials.

Publishing and accessing podcasts

There are two main ways in which the creator of a podcast can make them available for people to use, which is called publishing the podcast. The website that has the original podcast on it is called the 'host site'. The host site can be a university provided VLE or an open website. Similarly, there are two main ways that people receiving the podcast can get to know that it is ready and available for them: either as a direct notification such as an email or an announcement on the front page of the VLE, or via an internet 'feed'.

VLE hosting and direct publishing

If you are starting out as a podcast producer, the quickest and least technical way to publish your podcasts is to put them into your module on your VLE. We call this 'direct publishing' and it is very easy. They can be attached as an MP3 file in the same way as you attach your Word documents or PowerPoint slides.

Using the VLE means that the podcasts are delivered within a password-protected institutionally supported web service where access is enabled through an authentication process. However, with a VLE, you will then need to let your students know the podcasts are available one way or another. If your podcasts are in a series, sticking to a regular day of the week works well.

Internet hosting

If, however, you want to use the internet, outside the VLE, then read on. Internet 'feeds' for podcasts are available from most websites that offer current or changing content. Feeds allow the listener to see when websites have added something new. Feeds are known by the term 'RSS', which stands for 'Really Simple Syndication'. There are three main feed technologies in use but the commonest is RSS 2.0.

An RSS feed is a web file that groups information by themes on a web page and sends this information to people who have asked for updated information on specific topics. Such people are called 'subscribers'. You can think of this process rather like 'subscribing' to receive your favourite magazine or newspaper regularly for a period although RSS feeds are usually free.

Figure 1.1 RSS icon on a website

If a website is offering an RSS feed it will have the icon, with an orange background and white lines and a white dot, shown in Figure 1.1.

The RSS feed does not contain the content but provides links back to the original website where the material can be read (news article), viewed (TV/video) or downloaded and listened to – a podcast! The best ones to try first are news providers such as the BBC (bbc.co.uk) or *The Times* newspaper's sites (timesonline.co.uk). Both of these offers free RSS feed services and will help you to get the idea.

An RSS feed requires a piece of software called a 'reader'. Reader software checks the feeds and informs you of any new information such as a news item or podcast from the BBC. Clicking on the link in the Reader automatically connects you to the hosting service and the article is downloaded, letting you read the new article or listen to the podcast.

There are many different types of RSS readers: some are included with most web browsers and some are downloadable applications. With browser-based readers you can access your RSS feed subscriptions from your computer. Web browsers like Internet Explorer and Firefox both support the RSS feed readers where RSS feeds are stored in a similar way to 'favourites' within a browser.

Downloadable RSS readers are available for all PCs and the RSS feed will automatically update when you are connected to the internet. For example, the iTunes software checks the feed and downloads automatically any new material linked to the feed directly onto the subscriber's local computer.

Placing RSS feed readers onto a personal computer limits their use to that machine. People who want to access their feeds from various locations like to use web 'dashboard tools': one such example is Google Reader (google .com/reader) if you would like to try it out. Some people subscribe to many RSS feeds. They use tools that can manage and organize a large number of feeds. Two examples, iGoogle (www.google.com/ig/) and Netvibes (www.netvibes.com), are available free of charge.

Many of your students may be familiar with these methods for downloading their music.

Mixed hosting

Creating a feed can be daunting for the novice podcast creator, though it becomes quite easy with a bit of practice. Some feed services are now becoming available through VLEs. In Blackboard, for example, a feed service is provided by third-party software written by Learning Objects (learningobjects. com). This means that students can be alerted and linked to the new podcast. In this way, you can combine the advantages of posting course-specific podcasts on a password-protected VLE module and the subscribing and alerting services in common use on the internet.

It is not just a technical choice about where podcasts are stored and how they are distributed. Some lecturers are very happy for their words to be heard by anyone and storage of podcasts on internet services, such as iTunes, is then appropriate. Others prefer to distribute their podcast via the protection of institutional VLEs. And there are copyright issues – you need to check that you have the right to use the resources.

Podcasting as a learning technology

Table 1.2 shows seven technological aspects of podcasts that support learning. Here we compare them with pre-podcasting approaches.

Content capture

Developing conventional audio and video materials for learning and teaching purposes demands the booking of expensive sound and video recording studios and relies on the expertise of a range of technicians. Although the finished product of such a process is typically professional and of 'broadcast' quality, the cost, the time and other resources involved means that most academics are not able to make optimum use of such technology for their educational programmes.

By comparison, capturing and recording content for podcasts is a much simpler process and can be learned quickly by non-experts. The costs of provision and access are low. The simplicity of the technology was evident in our IMPALA project podcast development process. In IMPALA workshops, academics who had never used recorded sound and video for teaching were able to learn the basic technology of recording content, editing, finalizing and publishing podcasts. The longest workshops were about three hours and covered pedagogical and technological aspects of podcasting. The equipment involved was often their personal laptops that they also used for general academic work. If they had a digital sound recorder they could use it. Free software was downloaded from the internet – see this book's website for links (podcastingforlearning.com). Often the only extra hardware needed was a microphone and these are very cheap.

Table 1.2 Technical features of podcasting to support learning

Characteristic or feature to support learning	Earlier approaches	Podcasting approach
1. Content capture	Specialized equipment Recording studios	Computers, digital sound recorders Cheap equipment Free software and tools
2. Distribution mechanisms	Duplication/copying Postal services	RSS feeders – free and easy to use VLE delivery
3. Learner access	Postal services Collecting personally	RSS aggregators Downloads
4. Learner-owned personal devices	Cassette player Walkman	Portable mobile devices: MP3, MP4, phones, PDAs Wireless-enabled laptops
5. Technical skills	Training programmes Instructional texts and videos	Owners (students) already familiar with operations of devices
6. Context of learning and use	Bulky tapes, limitations, lack of flexibility	Ease of use, flexibility, mobility, near unlimited storage
7. Content contributors	Teachers, institutions	Teachers, students, alumni, non-specialists

Many participants in the IMPALA project either made their own podcasts and/or provided a small amount of support and training so that their students could create their own on locations away from the university. Development of video-based podcasts required more technical support. Even then, however, the process of development was simpler and less resource-intensive than developing conventional video and audio-vision programmes.

So our experience is that the technology is simple enough to put fairly quickly and easily into the hands of most university teachers. This transfer of power from technical specialists to the novice teacher makes a positive contribution to developing resources for student learning. The simple technology enables a university teacher to create podcasts at a time and locations suitable for him or her. Flexibility in terms of time and location enables lecturers to be informal and creative in the process of podcast development.

Distribution and access to podcasts

Receiving podcasts through a subscription service such as iTunes enables students to receive new audio material directly onto their desktop computers. Once the subscription service is started, the podcasts arrive automatically each time something new is available, until the learner cancels the service. Alternatively RSS aggregators (for example Google Reader) can make students aware that new podcasts are available to download.

If the VLE is used students are required to log into the course area when the podcasts are made available and manually download them onto their computer and/or their digital media player devices.

For novice academic podcasting, we endorse this simplified approach. Students are now increasingly getting used to visiting daily their course sites on the VLE, most of them more than once a day. Accessing podcasts manually will not hinder their use. If students are used to visiting the VLE regularly, and if the content is relevant, students will download and use them. Our questionnaire surveys of students who used IMPALA podcasts revealed that an overwhelming majority of them have access to the internet at their term-time accommodation, with nearly 90 per cent on high-speed broadband connections with unlimited access and the remainder split between pay-as-you-use high-speed and dial-up access. Only about 5 per cent of the students indicated that they did not have access to the internet in their term-time accommodation, but all have access to it at their university facilities. Interviews with students showed that they have sufficient access at university facilities so that they can transfer relevant files onto storage devices such as memory sticks, MP3 players and their laptops, to work on in their accommodation. Students will access and use podcasts that are purposeful, useful and relevant.

Learner-owned personal devices

IMPALA surveys in 2006 and 2007 confirmed that 90 per cent of students entering UK universities were equipped with one or more types of MP3 playback device. Nearly 30 per cent of these students had mobile phones with MP3 playback facility, 30 per cent had an iPod and a further 35 per cent had other brands of MP3 player. Podcasts can be played back on desktop and laptop computers that students have already bought for course-related and recreational purposes. Our IMPALA surveys revealed that a significant majority of students have their own laptop or a desktop computer. At one UK university 86 per cent of undergraduate students had access to a laptop computer and 11 per cent to desktop computers.

Mobile phones are being upgraded year by year with new features, so soon most students entering universities will have access to more than one type of device that can play back MP3 and/or MP4 files.

The characteristics of MP3 and MP4 players that make them appealing to large numbers of users also increase their potential for use for learning as well as entertainment. The IMPALA case studies confirmed that both learners and teachers valued the very large storage capacity on MP3 and MP4 players (and the storage can be extended by small additional storage cards), and they were aware that prices were dropping fast.

Most of the students' laptops come with software to enable access to the internet from wireless locations, further enhancing the potential for their use outside the formal classroom, including via wireless access points throughout the campus and while travelling.

Technical skills

The use of personally owned devices means that students are already familiar with their basic technical operation. It is rarely necessary to train them, as it is with other learning technologies such as VLEs. However, the transfer from using personal devices for entertainment to learning needs other kinds of motivation and support. Our companion book *Podcasting for Learning in Universities* gives you deeper insight into these.

Context of learning and use

The portability of podcasting offers the potential for students to access easy-to-use academic content and support from many locations:

- outside of the lecture theatre and seminar room in informal settings such as at home or in the library;
- away from the campus but in relevant locations for learning such as on the 'dig', in the field or at work;
- while carrying out everyday activities;
- while travelling.

A major factor that determines the context of using podcasts is whether they have been designed to be used along with formal learning activities or not. For example, to support fieldwork in Geography or Geology podcasts may be typically used in practical classes whereas study skills podcasts are often not directly linked to any classroom activity; therefore, they could be listened to at a time and place suitable to the learner.

Interviews with students who listened to podcasts outside classrooms revealed that they preferred to listen in the evenings when they were relaxing at home or in term-time accommodation. They were able to listen to podcasts without doing other learning-related activities such as taking notes. Student choice and the flexibility offered by podcasts was a key feature of podcasts that surfaced again and again in interviews with students who listened to podcasts. Unlike learning from a lecture in a classroom full of students, podcasts can shift the control over the pacing of learning activities from the teacher to the student, offering many options for flexibility.

Content contributors

The ease in creating podcasts makes a unique contribution to their use as learning resources. Podcasting promotes contributions from a wide range of groups and individuals. Beyond the obvious developers, such as university teachers, contributors may include:

- experts in the field;
- other academics;
- students;
- alumni;
- non-specialists;
- members of local or international communities.

By contrast, for the traditional use of audio and video in education the content was generated by subject specialists directly employed by and/or affiliated to the educational institution. Wide and creative contributions for knowledge-sharing, engagement and interest is a main feature of Web 2.0 technologies, of which podcasts are a part.

2

How to create podcasts – practitioner's guide

Matthew Mobbs, Gilly Salmon and Palitha Edirisingha

Summary

Here we provide a practical guide for producing podcasts. It covers technical aspects, such as equipment required, when to record podcasts, and editing and publishing your podcasts. It includes a section on copyright guidelines, if you are using material created by others.

Section 1: Equipment for podcasting

You will need a computer with a sound card, a microphone and speakers. Or instead of the microphone and speakers you can use a separately purchased 'headset' that includes both. You wear the headset.

The quality of the microphone determines the quality of the recording. There are many types and prices available. You will not need the highest quality for podcasting but it is worth spending a little more than the lowest price.

There are two main types of microphone connection to the computer: the 3.5 mm Phono Jack and those able to connect through the USB port.

The USB connector is less affected by connection problems and results in a much cleaner sound quality. A USB connection is also easier to plug in and use.

Section 2: Preparing to record

Undertaking some simple checks before you record will avoid technical problems.

The recording volume of the microphone can be adjusted using the audio controls on your computer. Figure 2.1 shows the microphone volume control for a Windows operating system. This can be accessed by selecting the

Figure 2.1   Windows microphone volume control

Control Panel on the **Start Menu** of your computer. Select **Switch to Category view** in the left hand menu pane, then select **Sound, Speech and Audio Devices**, followed by **Sound and Audio Devices**. From the **Volume** tab select **Advanced**. From **Options** menu, select **Properties** and chose to **Adjust Volume** for **Recording**. Then click **OK**. The **Record Control** window will appear where you can adjust microphone volume control (Figure 2.1).

If the volume setting is too low (demonstrated by a small sound wave on the audio recording software, labelled as 'Too Quiet' in Figure 2.2), the recording will be inaudible. If the setting is too high (represented by the sound wave going beyond the boundaries set in the audio software, similar to 'Too Loud' section in Figure 2.2), there will be some distortion of sound in the final recording.

For a good sound recording, the peaks of the sound wave should be within the tramlines as shown in Figure 2.2. We added these tramlines for your guidance; they are not a feature of the software. Keeping your recording within them will ensure that all sound is detected and be of audible levels. To achieve this, the microphone volume for your computer needs to be set correctly using either the **Volume Control** shown in Figure 2.1 or the **Audio Set-up Wizard**.

Experiment with the distance between your mouth and the microphone: increasing the distance will decrease the level of the recording volume; decreasing the distance will increase the volume.

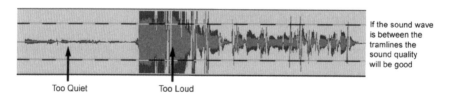

Figure 2.2   Recommended volume level in Audacity

Using your Voice

Tone of voice: A podcast made by a speaker with animated vocal expressions is more effective than a monotonous tone.

Umms and ahhs: A few are OK; no need to remove these during editing as long as the recording sounds natural.

Breathing noise: If your microphone is too close to your mouth, it may detect the sound of your breathing. A microphone attached to headphones is more likely to have this effect. The solution is to speak a little further away from the microphone.

Ambient sound

Ambient sound is picked up by the microphone. Prepare your environment: close windows, turn off your phone and put a notice on the door.

Section 3: Recording

Software

Several software packages, at a range of prices, are available for editing audio files. The IMPALA project found that free open source software is adequate: there was no need to buy expensive commercial software. IMPALA used Audacity downloaded from sourceforge.net. Audacity offered us the capabilities we needed to produce high-quality podcasts. We have used Audacity in the Appendix as an example. You can get Audacity from the link on the book's website: www.podcastingforlearning.com.

Audacity allows you to record multiple audio tracks that can be put together to create a seamless recording. Special effects editing tools, such as fade-in and fade-out, are also provided and are easy to learn to use.

Audacity supports advanced audio editing features including change-able sample rate frequency and export bit-rate (see Chapter 1, pp. 3–4) to vary the sound quality. Labels can be used to mark the sound track and to cut longer recordings into shorter individual tracks.

But Audacity does not have the in-built ability to create MP3 files. To achieve this, a free add-on to Audacity is needed. You need to download a small program, called lame_enc.dll, from the internet and install it on your computer. You can get 'lame_enc.dll' file from the link on the book's website: www.podcastingforlearning.com. Follow the installation directions. Make sure you do this before you start using Audacity.

Recording

After you have installed Audacity successfully on your computer, follow these steps.

1. Become familiar with the Audacity interface
When you first try Audacity, you need only use a few of the features. See Figure 2.3 below.

The icons on the **Control Toolbar** work in the same way as those on a video or audio cassette recorder (Table 2.1 opposite).

The **Meter Toolbar** is a measure of the decibel (volume) level of the microphone and output volume. The **Mixer Toolbar** adjusts the microphone input level and playback volume.

Four **Input Devices** can be used in Audacity: Microphone, CD Audio, Mono Mixer and Stereo Mixer. The microphone is required to record a podcast.

The **Time Rule** is a scale of time that represents the length of the recording. The **Timer Position** represents time within the recording where the cursor is positioned. This is mainly used in the editing process.

The **Sample Rate** figure represents how many samples of your voice the software records per second. This can be changed using the drop-down menu in Audacity. The higher the figure, the greater the quality of the recording and the higher the file size. The lower the figure, the poorer the quality of the recording but the saved file will be smaller.

2. Start recording
Set the **Input Device** as **Microphone**. Press **Record** and start speaking. As you talk, Audacity will produce a sound wave trace of your voice on the screen.

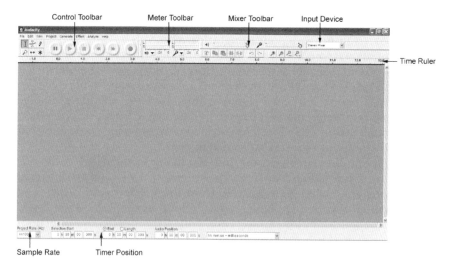

Figure 2.3   Becoming familiar with Audacity interface

Table 2.1 Audacity Control Toolbar icons

Figure 2.3a Icon of Record button on Audacity Control Toolbar

Record – initiates the recording of an audio file.

Figure 2.3b Icon of Pause button on Audacity Control Toolbar

Pause – temporarily stops the recording or playback. This is useful if you record one part of your podcast and then want to prepare yourself for the next section. To restart recording press the **Pause** button again.

Figure 2.3c Icon of Stop button on Audacity Control Toolbar

Stop – ends the recording or playback. This must be done before any further editing is carried out.

Figure 2.3d Icon of Play button on Audacity Control Toolbar

Play – plays back a recording.

Figure 2.3e Icon of Back button on Audacity Control Toolbar

Back Skip – skips to the beginning of the recording.

Figure 2.3f Icon of Forward button on Audacity Control Toolbar

Forward Skip – skips to the end of the recording or to a position where the cursor is placed.

Figure 2.3g Icon of Cursor button on Audacity Control Toolbar

The Cursor – This is a very useful tool that can be used either to select a certain position in a recording or to select a sample of the recording to be edited. We will look at this in more detail later in this chapter.

The **Meter Toolbar** will fluctuate according to the rise and fall of your voice level. The **Timer Positions**, at the bottom of the screen, will count the length of your recording. Some of these features can be seen in Figure 2.4.

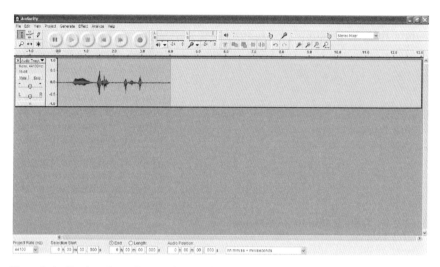

Figure 2.4   Testing the volume of an Audacity recording

When you press **Stop** an Audio Track summary with technical information will appear at the left-hand side of the sound wave. This is a function of the software that is useful for sophisticated editing; for example, in the music industry. You can ignore this feature when you are creating academic podcasts.

3. Listen
It is a good idea to play back and listen to your recording. It may feel a little strange to listen to your own voice if it is for the first time, but at this stage you are interested in the sound quality! If you think the recording is too loud you can adjust the record volume level by moving the tab on the **Microphone** section of the **Mixer Toolbar** (Figure 2.5). Experiment with different settings by adjusting this slider until it is at a level you consider acceptable.

Figure 2.5   Audacity mixer toolbar

4. Correcting mistakes
If you make a mistake you do not need to start again (see Figure 2.6). Be silent for about three seconds. This produces a flat line in the sound wave, which you can use to identify the mistake later. If you need time to compose

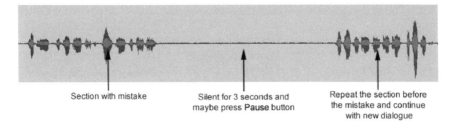

Figure 2.6 How to correct a mistake when recording

yourself, click on the **Pause** button to stop the recording until you are ready. Then click the **Pause** button again to continue recording by repeating the section leading up to the mistake and carry on.

You can then remove the mistake. Once you have clicked **Stop**, listen again to the section in which you made the mistake and decide exactly which part ought to be removed, by using measurements on the **Timer Position**. This may take a few attempts.

Once you have chosen the part to be removed, highlight the unwanted section, as shown in Figure 2.7, using the **Cursor** and the left-hand mouse button.

Figure 2.7 How to delete a mistake in a recording

To remove this section press the **Delete** key on your keyboard: the sound wave will realign itself and shorten the length of the recording by the amount of time removed.

5. Adding extra dialogue and sound tracks
If you miss something out, you can record the missing dialogue and insert it in the required location. See overleaf.

Position the cursor at the end of the current sound track and click the **Record** button. This will open a second **Audio Track**, as seen in Figure 2.8. Record your new piece and press the **Stop** button when you have finished it.

You can insert your newly recorded **Audio Track** into the original recording. First, position the **Cursor** line at the point in the recording where the second recording is to be inserted, as shown in Figure 2.9.

Go to the **Edit menu** on the **Menu Bar** and select the **Split** option. This creates a small gap in the recording, as shown in Figure 2.10.

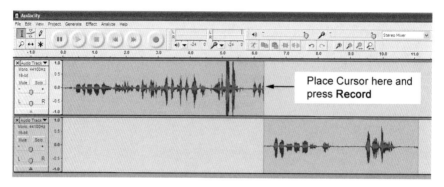

Figure 2.8   How to record extra dialogues and sound-tracks

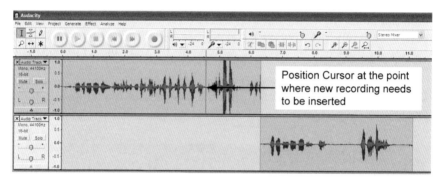

Figure 2.9   Position of the cursor at insert point

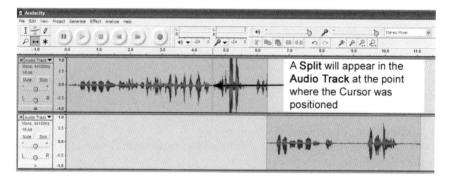

Figure 2.10   Creating a split in the audio track

Click on the **Time Shift** tool, as shown in Figure 2.11 and to be found on the **Control** toolbar. The cursor will change to a horizontal double arrow.

Hold the **Cursor** over the new audio track recording, click and hold down the left mouse button and move the recording to a position where the start of it is aligned with the split created above, as shown in Figure 2.12.

Figure 2.11   Time shift tool

Using the **Time Shift** tool, hold the **Cursor** over the sound wave to the right of the split in the original **Audio Track**, click and hold down the left mouse button and move **Audio Track**, position it at the end of the new recording in the second audio track, as shown in Figure 2.13.

The recording will now play back seamlessly with the newly recorded section inserted.

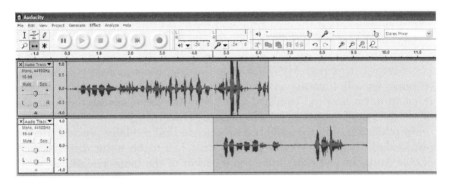

Figure 2.12   Positioning a new recording

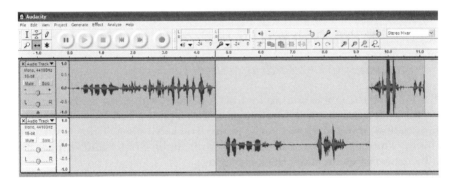

Figure 2.13   Positioning a previous recording

6. Save your podcast

To save your podcast, select **Save Project As . . .** from the **File Menu**. This option saves the recording as an **Audacity Project**, which is a format with the file extension **.aup**. The format can then be played back and re-edited but only using the Audacity software.

Now you need to convert the .aup file to MP3 format. To do this, from the **File Menu** select **Export As MP3**. This leads to a **Save** window, which prompts you to name your recording and select where you would like to store it on your computer. Complete these settings and click **OK**.

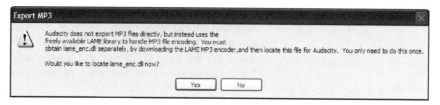

Figure 2.14 Warning message when lame_enc.dll is not located

Note, however, that the first time you try to do this conversion a warning message, as shown in Figure 2.14, will appear. This is because, as described in the Software section (p. 15) Audacity requires the **lame_enc.dll** plug-in to convert recordings to MP3 files. The warning message asks you to locate the **lame_enc.dll** file on your computer. The Software section provides information on how to download and install the **lame_enc.dll** file from the link on the book's web site: www.podcastingforlearning.com.

Now select **Yes**, and then use the browser to find the **lame_enc.dll** file you downloaded. This step of the process only has to be done the first time because Audacity will remember the location of the **lame_enc.dll** file every time you undertake this procedure after that. Audacity will now convert your recordings to an MP3 format.

Section 4: Publishing your podcasts

Personalizing your recording with ID3 Tags

ID3 Tags are the labels used to identify a podcast within the audio 'library' (or the collection of audio files) in your media player. ID3 Tags contain key information about podcasts such as the Track Number, Title, Artist and Album. The tags enable you to search your audio library and display the information when an audio track is playing.

The tags are important for keeping an audio library well organized, especially for students wishing to distinguish between their academic podcasts and music.

In Audacity once a recording has been saved as an MP3 file, the dialogue box shown in Figure 2.15 will appear. This is used to add ID3 Tags and assign them to your recording.

Initially, the **Edit ID3 Tags** option requires a **Format** to be chosen. There are two options: ID3v1 and ID3v2. We suggest you choose ID3v2.

Table 2.2 is a brief description of the tags that you can enter in the dialogue box, as shown in Figure 2.15.

It is not essential to use all the ID3 Tags. We recommend you use Title and Artist as these are the pieces of information that are critical for your students to identify their podcasts.

Figure 2.15 Audacity ID3 Tag editor

Table 2.2 Edit ID3 Tag labels

Title	The title of the episode of the podcast. If the podcast is one of a series it is good practice to put the number in the title (for example Show #12).
Artist(s)	The person(s) performing (talking on) the podcast.
Album	Here you put your overall theme.
Track Number	This is used to keep a series of podcasts in order, like the tracks on a CD. So label your podcast, 1, 2, 3, etc. in the series.
Year	The year the recording was produced.
Genre	We suggest 'Vocal' for educational podcasts.
Comments	This option can be left empty but you can use it to add any relevant information about the podcast; for example, any resources you referred to.

Figure 2.16 shows a completed example of the **Edit ID3 Tags** dialogue box for an IMPALA podcast. This one is for a recording in 2007 of student feedback. It also references the website.

If you want to change ID3 Tags later on, you can access the **Edit ID3 Tags** option at any time in Audacity from the **Edit Menu** by selecting **Edit ID3 Tags** and edit your Tags.

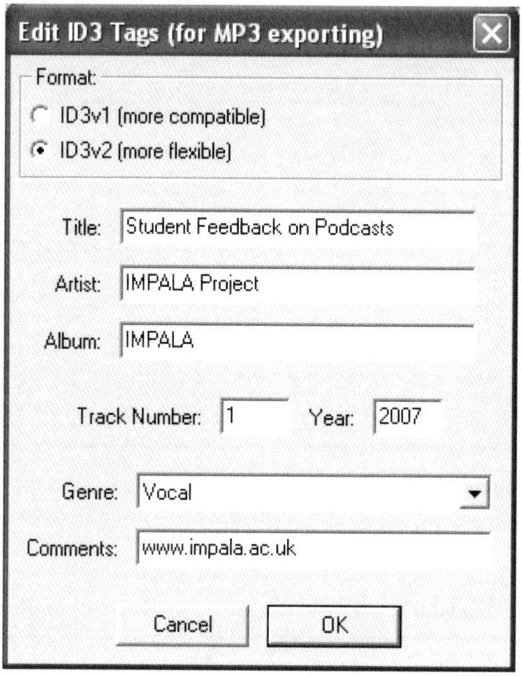

Figure 2.16   Example of a completed ID3 Tag editor

Enabling your podcast to be heard

Once a podcast has been produced you need to distribute it to your students. In order for your students to access your podcast, it needs to be stored online on a suitable server. You can place it on your Virtual Learning Environment (VLE) or institutional web server, or one of many websites that will host podcasts for you.

Podcasts and VLEs
If your VLE has a Content Management System (CMS), store your podcasts there as you will be able to refer to them from several places within your online course material.

If your VLE does not have a CMS, the file can be uploaded to the required place within the course module as you would any other file, giving it an appropriate name and a description. You may choose a separate area just for podcasts or store them alongside any other learning material.

When you are ready for your students to access your podcast, let them know by email that it is ready and where to find it. You can also make an announcement on the course message board. The message should encourage students to visit the course and download the podcast.

Soon VLEs such as Moodle and Blackboard will have Really Simple Syndication (RSS) tools that will allow students to subscribe to feeds, offering a full podcasting service, so keep track of the latest developments about your VLE!

Web-based podcasts

You may choose to put your podcast on a website so it can be freely accessed. There are several websites on the internet that offer a small amount of free storage space and then require a subscription for additional space. Those that offer free unlimited space sometimes include advertisements in your podcasts or they may limit the size of each upload.

Some free hosting websites available in January 2008 include:

- Big Contact – www.v2.bigcontact.com
- BT PodShow – www.btpodshow.com
- GCast – www.gcast.com
- iPod Networks – www.ipodnetworks.com
- My Podcast – www.mypodcast.com
- Odeo – www.odeo.com
- Podbean – www.podbean.com
- Podcast Spot – www.podcastspot.com
- Podomatic – www.podomatic.com
- Talkshoe – www.talkshoe.com
- Wildvoice – www.wildvoice.com

Other websites are listed at: www.okaytoplay.com/wiki/Podcast_Hosting.

Traditionally, an RSS feed is used to make subscribers aware of the availability of a new podcast. RSS is used to publish updates to web content that is regularly changed, such as blogs, news or podcasts. RSS is a 'web feed' with additional information about the content, and can be used to alert 'subscribers' to the feed, informing them of alterations or the availability of new content.

The symbols shown in Figure 2.17 are those used to show that an RSS feed is available for that content.

There are RSS capabilities on all the host sites listed above.

If you want to subscribe to them, copy the URL of the host site into an RSS aggregator. An aggregator is a 'feed reader' that picks up feeds from various websites and informs the subscriber of any updates to the content.

Figure 2.17 RSS symbols

The following RSS readers will inform you that a new podcast is available to download.

- NetVibes – www.netvibes.com
- Bloglines – www.bloglines.com
- Google Reader – www.google.com/reader
- My Yahoo – cm.my.yahoo.com
- News Is Free – www.newsisfree.com

These RSS aggregators actually download the newest podcasts for you. Two examples are:

- Juice – www.juicereceiver.sourceforge.net
- Doppler – www.dopplerradio.net

Once podcasts are downloaded, the students can open them or transfer them to suitable MP3 players as usual.

Publishing podcasts on iTunes
You can publish your own podcasts through iTunes. However, since iTunes does not physically store your podcasts, first you need to upload your podcasts to a hosting website with an RSS feed, such as those mentioned opposite. Now you need to tell iTunes where your podcasts are kept, by visiting the **iTunes Music Store** within iTunes software and selecting **Submit a Podcast** from the **Podcast** page shown in Figure 2.18, opposite.

Then enter the URL of your podcast hosting website into the submission screen shown in Figure 2.19 opposite.

Once submitted, the podcast will be available in the **iTunes Music Store** and the ID3 Tag information, along with a picture, will be displayed. An example of this is shown in Figure 2.20, on page 28.

Downloading podcasts from iTunes takes little effort. You can search the extensive library, and subscribe to a podcast that interests you. You can search the iTunes catalogue by keyword, title, theme or producer.

Figure 2.18 iTunes music store

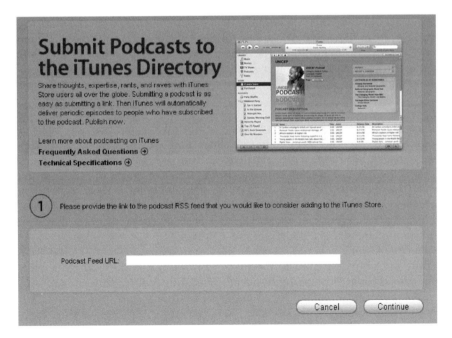

Figure 2.19 How to submit a podcast to the iTunes music store

Figure 2.20   Example of a podcast in iTunes music store

Once subscribed to, the iTunes aggregator automatically downloads the podcast and any subsequent episodes that are released later. Once downloaded, the podcasts are kept in the students' iTunes Library. Then the next time their iPod is connected iTunes will transfer them over to the portable device.

Section 5: Podcasts and copyright

We believe that the advice contained in this section to be accurate, but it does not constitute legal advice. If you are in any doubt as to whether or not you can use material, we recommend that you seek legal advice. Your institution's or organization's Copyright or Intellectual Property Rights officer will help you.

You may wish to include content that is not your own copyright, such as readings from literature or a script, or you may wish to make your podcast more creative by including music or sound effects. So you need to know a bit about copyright law and how it applies to podcasting. It is not difficult and if you know about it, it should not get in your way!

Copyright

Copyright law states that when a piece of work is created it is automatically copyrighted, even if a licence has not been applied for. Anyone who would like to use the work must seek permission from its creator before using it.

Some people are now making use of 'Creative Commons' on the internet, which has been introduced to allow the producer of a piece of work to inform others wanting to use it what rights they have. Creative Commons is a non-profit agency in the USA (www.creativecommons.org), that work internationally to make copyright more flexible.

Pieces of work covered by Creative Commons use a coding system to signify the rights assigned to the piece of work, which they call a 'licence'. You could consider assigning rights of use to your podcasts if you wish.

For more information on Creative Commons and podcasting, visit www.creativecommons.org, where you can find the 'Podcasting Legal Guide: Rule For The Revolution': (www.wiki.creativecommons.org/Podcasting_Legal_Guide).

Podsafe music

Podsafe music consists of pieces that have been released into the public domain, and can be reused and edited to fit the needs of anyone downloading it. You can use podsafe music freely in your podcast, perhaps as introductory music or to represent a section break in the recording.

In January 2008, these websites claimed to be offering podsafe music.

- Stockmusic.net – www.stockmusic.net
- Podsafe music network – www.music.podshow.com
- Podshow – www.btpodshow.com
- Podcast NYC – www.podcastnyc.net/psm/podcast.html
- Garage Band – www.garageband.com
- PodSafe Audio – www.podsafeaudio.com
- UK Podcasts – www.ukpodcasts.info
- People Sound – www.peoplesound.com
- Soundflavour – www.soundflavor.com

Published literature

In the academic world, we are used to referencing other people's work. However, with a podcast you should be especially careful because of the 'broadcast' element. Always ask permission of the copyright owner, who is not necessarily the same person as the author, if you want to use the work of others, whether from books, journal articles, websites or blogs.

Acknowledgement

Thanks to Dominic Mazzoni, project manager at Audacityteam.org, for his permission in our reproducing the screendumps of Audacity for this chapter.

Glossary

AAC   Advanced Audio Coding, file format supported by Apple.
Audio podcasts   podcasts containing sound only.

Enhanced podcasts   an extended version of audio podcasts capable of displaying additional information such as still images, weblinks and chapter markers.

GIS   Geographic Information System.

iPod   an Apple designed portable media player.

MP3   (MPEG Audio Layer III) a digital audio encoding format.
MP4   (MPEG-4 Part 14) a digital audio and video encoding format.
MPEG   Moving Picture Experts Group, established in 1988.

PDA   Personal Digital Assistant. A handheld device offering some functionality of a computer and may contain additional features such as a mobile phone, a music and/or video player and a camera.
Podcast   a digital media file available via a website.
Podcasting   the act of creating and distributing a podcast.

RSS   (Really Simple Syndication) a web feed format used to inform readers, listeners or viewers of new web content.

VLE   Virtual Learning Environment.
Vodcast/video podcast   a digital media file containing audio and video available via a website.
Vodcasting   the act of creating and distributing a vodcast.

Windows   a PC operating system developed and marketed by Microsoft.
Windows Mobile   a compact operating system developed by Microsoft and specifically designed to run on small handheld devices (PDAs).
WMA   Windows Media Audio file format.